Hooty Knows

Text & Illustration © 2015, Canadian Centre for Child Protection Inc.
615 Academy Road, Winnipeg, Manitoba, R3N 0E7

The Canadian Centre for Child Protection is a registered Canadian charity. Our goal is to reduce child victimization by providing programs and services to the Canadian public.

"**Hooty**" is a character created by the Canadian Centre for Child Protection, and "**Hooty Knows**" is one of a series of books that has been designed to complement the 7 Root Safety Strategies from the **Kids in the Know** program. "Hooty Knows" corresponds with the "If Asked to Go and Your Parents Don't Know. Shout No!" root safety strategy.

"Kids in the Know" is a safety program designed to empower children and reduce their risk of victimization. It focuses on building self-esteem through teaching critical problem-solving skills. The program uses an inclusive, community based approach to heighten safety awareness. The core premise of the program is based on key root strategies and environments which are reinforced and practiced throughout every grade level.

For more information on the Kids in the Know safety curriculum, visit **protectchildren.ca**.

Printed in Canada

ISBN # 978-1-927103-54-8 (English)
ISBN # 978-1-927103-55-5 (French)

October 2015

 CANADIAN CENTRE *for* **CHILD PROTECTION**® *Helping families. Protecting children.* is a trademark of the Canadian Centre for Child Protection Inc., registered in Canada.

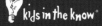 is a trademark of the Canadian Centre for Child Protection Inc., registered in Canada.

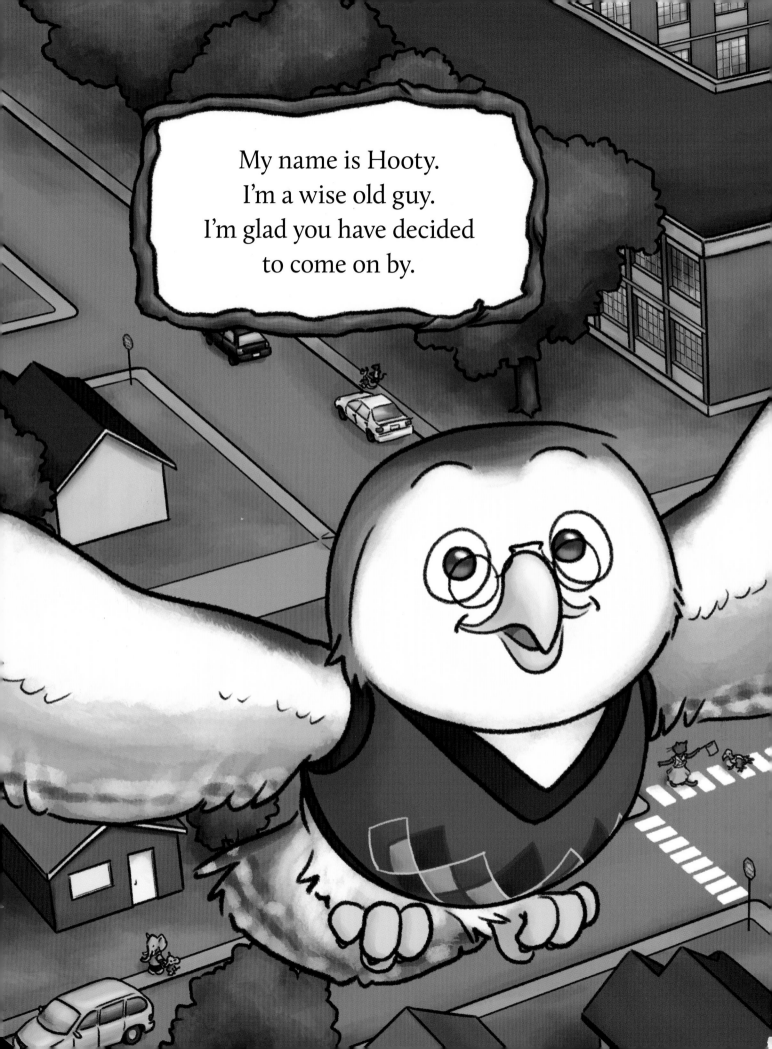

Hoo! Hoo!

Here come the kids that have left school.
Let's have a look at what is cool.
Off they walk with all the folk.
They're talking, laughing, and telling jokes.

When you're scared, you will get through.
But this is what you have to do:

When asked to go and
your parents don't know...

Use your eyes and your ears.
Trust your feelings of fear.
Turn away! Run! Go and tell someone!

If you're asked to go
and your parents don't know,

Shout NO!
Shout NO!

It could be adults, neighbours, friends,
Or the person around the bend.

Regardless of the presented excuse,
Always remember the words to use:

If you're asked to go and
your parents don't know,

Hip hip hooray! Hip hip hooray!
You're absolutely on your way!
You didn't go because you know,

If you're asked to go
and your parents don't know,

Shout NO!
Shout NO!

Hoo! Hoo!

Here's to you!
No matter what, you will get through.
Now you know just what to do!

The Canadian Centre for Child Protection (**protectchildren.ca**) is a registered charitable organization dedicated to the personal safety of children. We offer a number of programs, services and resources for Canadians to help them protect children and reduce their risk of victimization. This includes:

cybertip!ca®

Cybertip.ca is Canada's tipline for reporting the online sexual exploitation of children. Cybertip.ca also provides the public with information and other resources, as well as support and referral services, to help Canadians keep themselves and their families safe while using the Internet.

cybertip.ca

missing**kids**.ca™

MissingKids.ca is Canada's missing children resource centre. The program offers families support in finding their missing child and provides educational materials to help prevent children from going missing.

missingkids.ca

 kids in the know®

Kids in the Know is an interactive safety education program for children from kindergarten to high school. The program is designed to empower children and reduce their risk of victimization. It uses a community-based approach to heighten awareness of child safety and protection strategies.

kidsintheknow.ca

COMMIT TO KIDS®

Commit to Kids is a program to help organizations create safe environments for children. It provides strategies, policies, and a step-by-step plan for reducing the risk of child sexual abuse.

commit2kids.ca